A Straightforwar for Beginners

Nicholas Maynard

Straightforward Publishing
Brighton BN2 4EG

© Straightforward Publishing 2007

British Cataloguing in Publication data. A catalogue record is available
for this book from the British Library.

ISBN 1847160 07 7
ISBN 13 9781847160072

Printed in the United Kingdom by CPI Antony Rowe, Eastbourne

Cover Design by Straightforward Graphics

CONTENTS

Introduction   **7**

1 Types of Tiles in Use   **13**

2 Tools and Materials   **25**

Essential tools needed   25
Adhesives and grouts in use   30
Other materials   31

3 Tiling Walls   **33**

Different types of wall tiles   33
Preparing walls   36
Setting out wall tiles   41
Cutting and fixing   47

4 Tiling a Ceiling   65

Types of tile in use   65
Preparation   71
Setting out   71
Fixing tiles   72

5 Floor Tiles   **75**

Different types of floor tiles   75
The preparation of a floor   76
Setting out   78
Cutting and fixing   79

6 Useful Tips   **95**

7 Specialist Work   **103**

Caring for Victorian houses   103

Useful Addresses and Places to Visit   **117**

INTRODUCTION

The use of clay tiles to protect and decorate walls and floors is very old indeed. Evidence from the earliest settlements demonstrates the use of this material for basic insulation and decoration. However, medieval monasteries developed the art of tile making to a high degree. Their complex inlaid tile pavements inspired many later Victorian designers.

Monastic tile making came to an end with the dissolution of the monasteries. In most domestic interiors the use of tiles was unknown until the seventeenth century, when plain quarry tiles were used for floors – but only in the better houses; most dwellings still had earth floors.

Hand painted glazed tiles were imported from Holland in the eighteenth century and a few English tile works were set up to imitate this fashionable "Delft" ware. In 1756, a patent was granted for a transfer printing process that increased production of decorated glazed tiles, but it was not until 1830, when the porcelain manufacturer Herbert Minton began to invest in tile production, that the astonishing growth of the nineteenth century industry began.

Victorian tile manufacturers found that the market for mass produced tiles was insatiable. Since they were cheap to obtain and easy to install, tiles offered the speculative builder the chance to incorporate cheerful, hygienic and fashionable decoration into all kinds of houses. New building regulations, requiring greater attention to hygiene, stimulated demand even further. By the mid 19th century, tile decoration of some kind was to be expected in even modest artisan dwellings.

The general enthusiasm for tiles became so great that in 1878 the "Pottery and Glass Trades Review" asked: "To what use can tiles not be put? Cornices and chair mouldings, door frames and windows are set with them; hearths outlined or made wholly from them, doors inlaid, and staircases decorated... summerhouses are gay with them, for the tile is always fresh and cool looking in its bright designs, while nothing is warmer for winter rooms than the dark earth coloured ones".

Today, most decorating materials are available in tile form. As well as the enormous ranges of ceramic tiles, there are mirrored, glass, cork, plastics, aluminium, stainless steel, vinyl, rubber and carpet. Although this book will cover the whole range of tiles in use, it is intended more for those who wish to undertake jobs using ceramic or other earth tiles in projects which require skill and patience.

Tiling techniques are the same for all materials except for the method of cutting them and adhesives for fixing them. Tiles are easier to handle than sheet materials, and actually fixing them onto walls and floors is simple. The one main problem is that the first tile determines the position of every other. This is where do–it–yourself tiling can be spoiled before it has even begun. The secret is to plan the entire job before fixing that first tile. This is called "setting out".

The main area of the wall or floor is called the "field" and is always tiled first with whole, uncut tiles. This leaves the spaces around the edges, called the "border" to be tiled separately, each tile being cut to fit. A well done job has a well balanced appearance, as though the tiles fell into place quite naturally and without effort. However, this is the result of spending as much time setting out the job as in fixing the tiles.

Tiling, perhaps more so than any other forms of decorating or general home D.I.Y. requires attention to detail and a great deal of patience. Quite often it will require a significant amount of money too. Therefore, anyone brave enough to consider a project such as the tiling of a whole bathroom, kitchen or hallway needs a good basic grounding into the techniques required to carry out a successful tiling job. Certainly, if you intend to carry out a more elaborate job, such as a patio or swimming pool, then you will need to have undertaken a smaller, easier project first.

This book is set out logically, enabling you to progress step by step until the necessary skills have been acquired to carry out tiling work. The chapters are arranged as follows:

Chapter One gives an overview of the types of tiles in use. It is very important to understand the type and nature of different tiles. The end result of your endeavour will very much depend on the materials used.

Chapter Two deals with the essential tools needed for the job and also gives an outline of the types of material needed in the tiling process. However, specific manufacturers are not mentioned, other than those makers whose names are the same as a product.

Chapter Three describes, in more depth, the process of wall tiling and the types of tiles used. The processes of preparation of surfaces and setting out are discussed, along with the art of shaping and fixing tiles and the process of "grouting".

Chapter Four deals with ceiling tiles and the process of fixing ceiling tiles, along with types of tile used.

Chapter Five deals with floor tiles. Floor tiles, along with wall tiles, are perhaps the most complicated processes and demand more attention to detail. In this chapter we look in more depth at the type of tile used and at the preparation of floors. We also look at setting out tiles and cutting and fixing. Finally we look at grouting of tiles.

Chapter Six puts forward a number of useful tips relating to previous chapters.

Chapter Seven looks at the care and restoration of Victorian tiles and covers the types of tile in use in that period. This is in recognition of the importance of restoration and conservation of homes and other buildings of this period.

There is a list of useful addresses which the reader can contact for further information concerning tiling.

Remember, tiling requires patience and attention to detail, and not a little money. The end result however, can be spectacular and a source of deep satisfaction to the person who has achieved the finish. Whether it be a kitchen or bathroom, a hallway or external work, or even a tiny project, an immense amount of pleasure can be gained.

GOOD LUCK!

1

.

TYPES OF TILES IN USE

This chapter looks at the different types of tiles in use and describes their different applications.

1 CERAMIC TILES

These tiles, available in glazed or matt finishes, are manufactured in many countries throughout the world and can be used for floors or walls. The majority of tiles are square but dimensions vary according to use and the manufacturers preference. Rectangular and more irregular shapes are also available. Typical shapes include Hexagons, Octagons, Diamonds and interlocking units with curved elaborate edges. Other units include slim rectangles with pointed or slanted ends. Use them in combination to produce patterned floors and walls.

Unglazed tiles are only normally used to provide a surer grip for flooring. A textured surface reduces the risk of accidents, especially where a floor might become wet. All ceramic tiles are durable and waterproof, however you should use heat resistant tiles where they are near hot places or frost resistant where they are likely to be used outside.

2 FIELD TILES

The single coloured (i.e. plain) base tile is commonly referred to as the field tile. Some designers use, as the base, a patterned or textured tile. For simplicity this can also be referred to as the field tile.

3 MOSAICS

The majority of mosaic tiles are ceramic and are purchased in sheets of approximately 300mm x 300mm. For individual mosaics of say 50mm x 50mm, there would be 36 individual tiles, correctly spaced, on a sheet. The sheets are held together by a nylon mesh that has been stuck to the back of the tiles. For speed of fixing, whole sheets can be adhered in a single operation rather than positioning every small tile individually. Mosaics are commonly used on walls, floors and worktops as well as being a popular cladding material for swimming pools.

Some mosaics are made from vitreous glass and are also supplied in sheets of approximately 300mm x 300mm. They are held together by being stuck onto gummed paper. A sheet of paper covers the face of the tiles and is removed by washing after the sheets have been fixed.

TYPES OF TILE IN USE

The examples shown left are a typical cross-section of commercially available ceramic tiles

1. Glazed ceramic
2. Shaped and size variation
3. Mosaic tiles
4. Quarry tiles
5. Slate and stone

CORK TILES

MINERAL FIBRE TILES

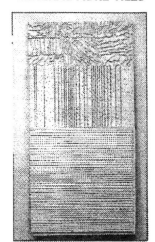

RUBBER TILES

POLYSTYRENE TILES

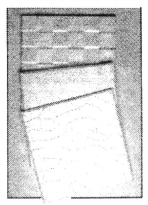

MIRROR/METAL TILES

For the more creative tiler, many individual designs can be achieved by working with mosaics. Materials that can be purchased in loose pieces for this purpose include venetian smalti, gold leaf on glass and coloured glass mosaic. Also, certain special effects such as "Roman Key" borders and decorative murals can be purchased ready made from specialist suppliers.

4 QUARRY TILES

Quarry tiles are thick, extremely hardwearing unglazed ceramic tiles used specifically for floors. As they take a lot of "foot traffic" they need a hardwearing waterproof surface. Colours are generally limited to browns, reds, black and white. Although they are manufactured in various sizes, the 6" x 6" tiles are normally specified. Quarry tiles are often referred to in error as "terracotta" but they are distinct from terracotta (see below) but provide a similar effect, i.e., a "farmhouse type" floor.

5 STONE AND SLATE FLOORING

Real or natural stone or slate tiles (marble, limestone, slate, granite and venetian marble) can be beautiful but expensive. Quite often used for floors, sizes and shapes will vary according to the manufacturer – some will even cut to measure. A few materials are so costly that you should consider using a professional to lay them, otherwise use quarry tiles.

The above are natural materials that have been quarried from the ground before being shaped and dressed to be supplied as tiles. Sealing and regular maintenance is required. Another natural tile,

"Encaustic" tile, made from natural stone strengthened with powdered marble, also requires sealing and regular maintenance. These tiles, available in plain colours as well as traditional patterns, can be used to create an "antique" style floor.

6 STONE AND BRICK TILES

Thin masonry can be used to simulate a stone or brick wall as a feature area for a chimney breast, for example, or to clad a whole wall. Stone tiles are typically made from reconstituted stone in moulds, and most look unconvincing as an imitation of the real thing.. Colour choice is intended to reflect local stone types, and is typically white, grey or buff. Some weathered versions are also made. Brick tiles look much more authentic. The best ones are actually "brick slips" – slivers cut from kiln-produced bricks. A very wide range of traditional brick colours is also available.

7 TERRACOTTA TILES

Terracotta or earthenware floor tiles have long been popular due not only to their mellow appearance but also to their ability to adapt to ambient room temperatures. Whereas, for example, glazed ceramic or quarry tiles remain cold, terracotta tiles can hold warmth as well as looking warm.

Terracotta tiles are often characterised by marks, chips, lime pops, cracks and even paw prints. They are ideal materials for creating the "traditional-look" floor. These tiles are available not only in various shapes and sizes, but also in different finishes.

It is worth sifting through your delivery of terracotta to see if you are "lucky" enough to have been supplied with tiles with paw imprints. The "saltillo" range of tiles often come with a few of these imperfections. These have been caused by cats running over the tiles in the drying yard before they have properly set. These tiles can be fixed so as to show a trail of pawprints across the floor!

If terracotta is specified, it must be noted that these tiles have to be sealed and polished as well as being regularly maintained. These steps will be clarified in a later chapter.

8 HANDMADE TILES

Tiles for walls, floors and worktops can be specified that have been produced using traditional hand production methods. Unlike machine manufactured ranges, these tiles are normally uneven in surface texture and are supplied with what could be described as imperfections. What should be remembered is that no two tiles are identical, so do not be alarmed if your tiles vary in size. You should check with your local supplier as to the suitability of these tiles for walls, worktops etc. Handmade tiles will be expensive so be very careful when you apply them.

9 VINYL TILES

Vinyl tiles are among the cheapest and easiest floorcovering to use. Vinyl can be cut easily, and so long as the tiles are firmly glued, with good joints, the floor will be waterproof. However, it will still be susceptible to scorching. A standard coated tile has a printed pattern between a vinyl backing and a harder, clear vinyl surface.

Solid vinyl tiles are made entirely of the hardwearing plastic. Some vinyl tiles have a high proportion of mineral filler. As a result they are stiff and must be laid on a perfectly flat base. Unlike standard vinyl tilers, they will resist some rising damp in a concrete sub floor. Most tiles are square or rectangular but there are interlocking shapes and hexagons. There are many patterns or colours to choose from, including embossed vinyl which represents ceramic, brick or stone tiling.

10 RUBBER TILES

Soft rubber tiles were originally made for use in shops or offices, but they are equally suitable for the home, being hardwearing but soft and quiet to walk on. The surface is usually studded or textured to improve the grip. Choice is limited to a few plain colours.

11 MIRROR TILES

Square and rectangular mirror tiles can be attached to walls with self adhesive pads in each corner. There is a choice of silver, bronze or smoke grey finish. Don't expect tiles to produce a perfect reflection unless they are mounted on a really flat surface.

12 METAL TILES

Lightweight pressed metal tiles are fixed in the same way as mirror tiles. Choose from aluminium, bronze and gold coloured tiles with satin or bright finishes. These tiles are not grouted so do not use them where food particles can gather in the crevices.

13 POLYSTYRENE TILES

Although expanded polystyrene tiles will not reduce heat loss from a room by any significant amount, they will deter condensation as well as mask a ceiling in poor condition. Polystyrene cuts easily so long as the trimming knife is very sharp. For safety in case of fire, choose a self extinguishing type and do not overpaint with an oil paint. Wall tiles are made, but they will crush easily and aren't suitable for use in a vulnerable area. There are flat or decoratively embossed tiles.

14 CORK TILES

Cork is a popular covering for walls or floors. It is easy to lay with contact adhesive and can be cut to size or shape with a knife. There is a wide range of textures and warm colours to choose from. Pre–sanded but unfinished cork will darken in tone when you varnish it. Alternatively, you can buy ready finished tiles with various plastic and wax coatings. Soft granular insulating cork is suitable as a decorative finish for walls only. It crumbles easily, so should not be used where it will be exposed on external corners.

15 MINERAL FIBRE TILES

These tiles, along with polystyrene tiles, are normally used for ceilings and are made from compressed mineral fibre. They are dense enough to be sound and heat insulating. They often have tongue and grooved edges so that, once stapled to the ceiling, the next interlocking tile covers the fixings. Fibre tiles can also be glued directly to a flat ceiling. A range of textured surfaces is available.

16 CARPET TILES

Carpet tiles have advantages over wall to wall carpeting. There is less to fear when cutting a single tile to fit, and, being loose laid a worn burnt or stained tile can easily be replaced. However, you cannot substitute a worn tile several years later, as the colour will not match. Buy several spares initially and move them around regularly to even out the wear and colour change.

Most kinds of carpet are available as tiles, including cord, loop and twist piles in wool as well as a range of man made fibres. Tiles are normally plain in colour but some are patterned to give a striking grid effect. Some tiles have an integral rubber underlay.

The above has given an exhaustive description of the various types of tiles in use. I have been careful to include the softer wall and ceiling tiles, although I realise that the majority of people buying this book will be interested in undertaking the more project based, ceramic tile, work. Therefore, in the following chapters, emphasis will be placed on this type of material and how to achieve an effective finish. However, I will touch on the laying of softer tiles.

In the next chapter, we will look at the all important area of tools and materials needed to carry out tiling work. As we progress, emphasis will be placed on the use of these tools.

STONE AND BRICK TILES

VINYL TILES

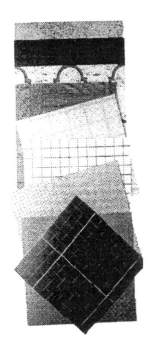

CARPET TILES

2

TOOLS AND MATERIALS

In order to carry out a tiling job effectively, a number of essential tools are needed. With tiling, you are only as good as the tools you have. In turn, you must know how to use them.

FINDING YOUR LEVEL

An accurate spirit level is essential for planning the layout (setting out) of tiles on walls and also determining the slope of floors. It is vital that you have a smooth and even surface when you begin the tiling job.

CHALK LINE

This is a reel of non stretch string that is used to make straight lines on walls, floors and ceilings. To "snap" a chalk line, fasten one end to a nail (or get a helper to hold it) on one mark, and hold it taut to the second mark. Then pull the line away from the surface and let it snap back. There will be a straight line of chalk between the two marks.

PLUMB LINE

This is a string with a weight on the end that, hanging free, shows a true vertical. It can be rubbed with chalk and used as above.

GAUGE STICK

This is a setting out tool you make yourself. Lay out a row of tiles, being sure to space them as they will be when fixed. Simply butt self spacing tiles together. Then place a batten next to the tiles and mark it at the corner of each tile. Use the gauge stick by placing it against the wall or floor to find the best position for the rows of tiles.

SCRIBER

This is used to set out floor tiles. It is easy to make yourself, as it is simply a batten approximately one metre long with a nail driven through both ends, so that the points protrude.

TILE CUTTERS

There are several types of proprietary tile cutters. The most common resembles pliers with two "wings" and also a wheel used to score

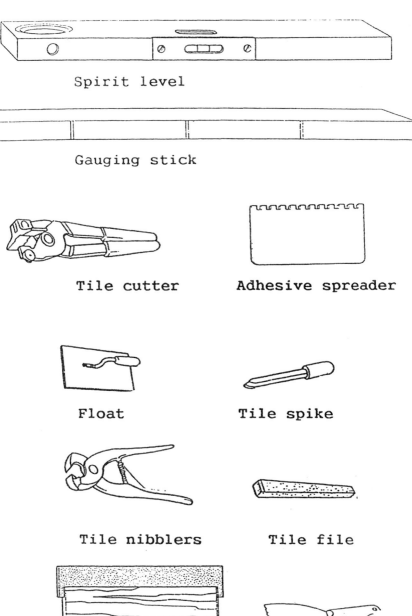

Spirit level

Gauging stick

Tile cutter

Adhesive spreader

Float

Tile spike

Tile nibblers

Tile file

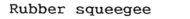

Rubber squeegee

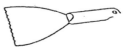

Filling knife

the tile. The jaws are used to snap the tile on the line. For cutting floor tiles, its best to hire a steel tile cutter. It generally costs more but will save on shattered tiles.

ADHESIVE SPREADERS

These are plastic or metal trowels with notches on the edge. They apply adhesive in even ridges and so help to avoid thick or thin patches. Often they are supplied free with the adhesive.

FLOAT

This is a rectangular metal or wooden plate with a handle on the top. It is used for spreading screed or laying sand and cement mortar on the floors.

TILE SPIKE

This is a traditional tool for scoring the line where a tile is to be cut. This creates a weak point, making it possible to break the tile along the line.

TILE NIBBLERS

These are pincers that are used to break off small pieces of tile, "nibbling away" the waste on an awkward shape.

TILE BREAKING BOARD

This is a flat piece of wood which is helpful to snap the tiles once they are scored. You can place matchsticks under the line at each edge, or for better results, fix a piece of bare wire across it. This supports the full width of the tile, giving a better chance of breaking it on the line.

TILE FILE

The best tool for smoothing the cut edges of ceramic tiles is a carborundum file, made of the same material as a knife sharpening stone. In fact, a stone can be used, although its not as good for getting into small places.

RUBBER SQUEEGEE

This is used to spread grout over the tiles and into the joints, using a thin rubber wiper with a handle of the kind used to clean windows. Its quicker than a sponge.

FILLING KNIFE AND SCRAPER

These look similar, but have different functions. The scraper is stiff and is used to remove wallpaper and flaking paint. The filing knife is flexible and is used to apply filler to cracks and holes in walls and ceilings.

BONDING AGENT

When sealing cement floors or to help new cement to bond to old, you should use a polyvinyl acetate adhesive diluted with water.

SELF LEVELLING COMPOUND SCREED

This is a water or resin based compound that is mixed to a creamy consistency and poured over slightly uneven floors. It doesn't require skill in smoothing the surface because it finds its own level and flattens out.

ADHESIVES

Don't try using the wrong tile adhesive for the job. Most ceramic tile adhesives are sold ready mixed although a few need to be mixed with water. Tubs or packets will state the coverage. The manufacturers always state which one to use for walls and which for floors. You must always use a flexible adhesive whenever tiling a surface that may have some movement, such as chipboard, hardboard or plywood sheets.

There are frost proof adhesives for use outside and heat resistant for work surfaces and fire places, and for surfaces that are often underwater, such as a shower, you must use a waterproof adhesive.

CONTACT ADHESIVE

If the manufacturer recommends fixing cork tiles with contact adhesive, use a water based (rather than solvent based) one. These are much easier to apply and have no heavy inflammable fumes.

GROUT

Grout is used to seal the joints between tiles, and to provide a finish. As with adhesives, the material in the joints between tiles must be flexible, frost proof, heat–resistant, or waterproof as the situation demands. Also, on tiled work surfaces where food is prepared, use a non toxic grout.

FILLER

This is used for surface repairs and comes in powder form to be mixed with water, or ready to use. Modern resin based fillers are better than cellulose fillers as they dry without shrinking, so cracks and holes can be filled flush.

SILICONE CAULK

This is available in tubes, in various colours, and is a mastic making a water tight joint between bath tubs and basins and the tiles. It remains flexible enough to accommodate movement. It also provides a good way of sealing the join between floor tiles and wall tiles.

The above is a list of tools and material that you need to equip yourself with in order to carry out an effective job. In the next Chapter, we discuss the tiling of walls and lay the foundations for tiling which you can then use in all your future jobs.

3

TILING WALLS

In chapter one, we discussed the different types of tiles in use. In this chapter we will be looking at the techniques employed when tiling a wall. There are a number of different tiles for use on a wall, each giving a different finish. Ceramic tiles for use on walls are available from many sources in vast ranges of colours, designs and sizes. Surfaces may be as smooth as glass or textured and matt. In fact the surface of glazed tiles is glass, making them a practical, hardwearing surface.

As well as different finishes, tiles may have different properties according to the use for which they are meant. As mentioned, some tiles are heat–resistant while others are frost proof. Modern ceramic tiles have lugs on the edges to take the effort out of keeping them uniformly spaced. Square tiles with unfinished edges are called "field tiles". However, where tiles meet on external corners, there are special tiles that are used to finish the edges. The traditional tiles for this are called "round edged" (RE) which have a round finished edge, and "double round edge" (REX) with two adjacent finished edges. These tiles are laid to cover the edges of the field tiles.

To finish the edge of field tiles on a flat surface, such as the top row of a half tiled wall, there are "Quadrant" tiles. These are like a narrow strip of a round edged tile. They can help give an authentic look to traditional patterns and antique tiles. Another type of edge finishing tile is sometimes called a "universal tile". These usually have two glazed edges.

As we have seen, mosaics are supplied in sheets of equally spaced pieces (known as "chips") making them as easy to fix as tiles.

Plastic tiles are made from thin plastic sheet to imitate ceramic wall tiles. Although they aren't as strong as ceramic tiles, their surface is warmer and they are very easy to fix, usually with self adhesive pads. Their main disadvantage is that they cannot withstand heat, so don't use them near cookers or fireplaces.

Cork, rubber, vinyl and carpet tiles may be used on walls, although cork is the most usual. The attraction of these materials, apart from their appearance, is that they are warm to the touch and also help to reduce noise by absorbing, rather than reflecting it. The advantage of using them in tile form is that waste is kept to a minimum.

Cork is available in different qualities for floors and walls. The floor tiles are compressed to increase their density. Wall tiles come in different thicknesses and densities. Unfinished cork can be finished with two coats of clear polyurethane or (on walls) left natural.

Cork tiles are available in various natural shades and some tiles have a slight grain direction that can be used to create a pattern.

A word of warning about cork tiles, however. Once they are on, they are there to stay. If there is a sudden and urgent need to remove them, because of a burst pipe for example, then you will not only have difficulty but you will make a mess of the overall tiling effect. You should keep this in mind when thinking of using cork tiles.

Metal tiles are fixed with pads in the same way as plastic ones. They are usually fixed butted together (without grouting) and provide a heat resistant and washable surface, although splash marks must be cleaned regularly. The aluminium ones usually cut easily with scissors, but you may need tin snips for stainless steel tiles. A major feature of metal tiles is that they can be bent around internal and external corners.

Mirror tiles are simply mirrored glass cut into tiles. The most important thing to remember is that the surface to which they are fixed must be absolutely flat and smooth. Any unevenness will cause a distorted reflection. One way to overcome this is by fixing plywood or chipboard to the wall. As mirror tiles are butted together without grout, its a good idea to lay them out first on a flat surface. They may not be exactly square and there can be some variation in size.

With all tiles, the quality of the job is decided at the planning stage. It takes as long to find the best arrangement, both for working out a pattern and to give the overall job a professional symmetry, as to actually fix the tiles.

THE PREPARATION OF WALLS

Whatever tiles you plan to use, the walls must be clean, sound and dry. You cannot tile over wallpaper, and flaking or powdery paint must be treated first to give a suitably stable base for the tiles. It is important that you make the surface as flat as possible so that the tiles will stick firmly. Setting out the prepared surface accurately is a vital aid to hanging the tiles properly.

NEW PLASTER

If you have recently plastered a surface, then new plaster needs at least one month to dry out before it can be tiled. Remove any little splashes (small bumps) of plaster and fill any cracks or dents. Then prime with a plaster primer or any universal primer to create a non absorbent surface for the tile adhesive.

FILLING CRACKS AND DENTS

This is carried out with a flexible filling knife and filler. Scoop some filler on to the end of the knife and press the blade flat over the fault, sliding away to leave the filler in the hole.(1)(Overleaf) You may need several attempts to ensure the filler is pushed right to the bottom without air being trapped underneath (if the filler bulges out of the hole there is an air bubble under it).

When you have applied enough to fill the hole, hold the knife almost vertically and scrape across the top to remove the excess.(2) Try to clean all the surplus away (including the ridges round the edges) leaving the repair flush. Its worth the extra time spent on the wet

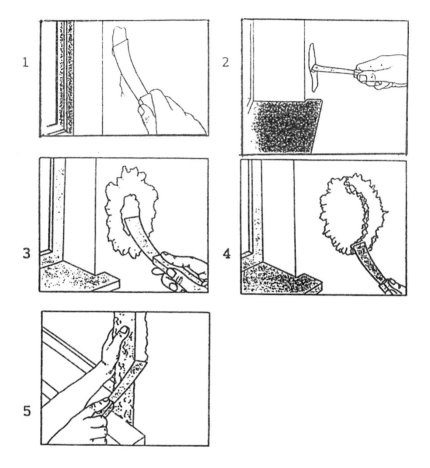

filler as rubbing down afterwards is messy, time consuming and hard work.

Large deep holes should be filled in layers not more than 3mm thick.(3) These dry quickly enough that you can apply a layer every so often while dealing with other small repairs.

Filling with thin layers helps with faults that are wider than the filling knife.(4) The surface is built up gradually around the edges, reducing the area to be scraped off flush. Remember to clean the surplus from around the edges each time you fill. Very large areas of damaged plaster should be repaired with plaster or one of the DIY plastering systems that is applied by brush. These are used in layers up to 3mm thick and take 24 hours to dry between coats so, if the fault is deeper than this, use ordinary filler to build up the surface until only a "skim coat" is needed. Keep working the surface (re-wetting if necessary) until you are satisfied with the finish

To get a neat edge on outside corners, hold a polythene wrapped piece of wood against one side and flush with the edge.(5) Fill the gap as if it were a crack. Then slide the wood away when the filler begins to set. Use a damp sponge to remove traces of wet filler.

WALLPAPER

Wallpaper or other wall coverings cannot be tiled. It is necessary to strip off all layers of old paper to reveal the plaster. Do this either by the "soak and scrape" method, as described below, or use a steam stripper.

When removing wallpaper, firstly check whether the paper is of the "peel off" variety by grasping a corner and pulling. Vinyl tiles are easily removed like this, but they leave the paper back on the wall. This must be removed in the normal way. To remove other wallpapers, begin by scoring the surface with a stiff wire brush. This is particularly important with washable (i.e. water-resistant) papers and those that have been painted over.

Next, fill a bucket with warm water and add a little vinegar (this reduces the surface tension and helps it to penetrate the paper). Using a large paint or pasting brush, soak the paper as much as possible. Use a stiff scraping knife to get under the paper, but be careful not to dig into the surface of the plaster. Keep re-soaking until the paper comes off easily. After stripping, wash off any traces of old adhesive with clean water.

For stubborn papers, try one of the chemical wallpaper stripping products instead of water and vinegar. These cling to the surface and allow more time for the adhesive to soften.

PAINTED WALLS

Gloss paint must be rubbed down with medium grade abrasive paper to key the adhesive. Matt finish paint needs to be washed and rinsed. Use a scraper to remove any loose paint and then fill as plaster. Remember to prime any bare areas or filler.

OLD CERAMIC TILES

Existing tiles may be tiled over if they are firmly stuck and any cracks filled. If the old tiles are glazed, rub them down with a coarse grade silicone carbide paper to scratch the surface lightly. This will help "key" the surface for the adhesive. Then wipe the surface with a cloth dampened with white spirit to remove any dust or old polish.

BRICK OR ROUGH CONCRETE

Uneven masonry walls will have to be plastered or rendered or lined with chipboard or plywood.

WOOD

Timber is not a suitable surface for tiles because the boards move in relation to each other. On a smooth wood wall, you can fix sheets of thin hardboard as described in the "floors" section of this book. However, if the wall seems unstable, its best to line it with plywood or chipboard sheets that are fixed to battens. Then it must be sealed with primer.

HOW TO LINE WALLS

To make a smooth stable surface for tiling, you can fix plywood or chipboard sheets to battens. Screw battens to the wall not more than 30cm apart. Fix the first one at the corner. Using the width of the sheets, calculate the other battens to be spaced equally, with a batten at the join with the next sheet. The last sheet on the wall will probably need to be cut to fit.

If there is a window or door, fix battens around the edges. Cut the sheets to fit the area to be tiled. Use a long straight piece of wood to keep the battens straight and parallel with each other. If necessary, use pieces of wood to space some battens away from the wall.

When all the battens are up, mark their positions on the sheets and screw the sheets to the battens. Prime the wood with an oil based primer to create a non absorbent surface and to prevent rust on the screw heads.

SETTING OUT WALL TILES

Setting out the prepared surface accurately is a vital aid to hanging the tiles properly. Its important that you make the surface as flat as possible so that the tiles stick properly.

MAKING A GAUGE STICK

One of the first tasks in setting out wall tiles is that of making a gauge stick. This is a tool for plotting the position of tiles on the wall. You should make this from a length of 50mm times 12mm softwood. You should position several tiles along it, butting together those with lugs, or add spacers for square edged tiles, unless they are intended to be close butted. Mark the position of each tile on the softwood batten. (See overleaf)

SETTING OUT A PLAIN WALL

On a plain wall, use the gauge stick to plan horizontal rows starting at the bottom (skirting) level. If you are left with a narrow strip at the top, move the rows up half a tile width to create a wider margin. You should then mark the bottom of the largest row of whole tiles. Nail a thin guide batten to the wall aligned with the mark. Make sure it is horizontal by placing a level on top.(1)

Mark the centre of the wall (2) then use the gauge stick to set out the vertical rows at each side of it. If the border tiles are less than half a width, reposition the rows sideways by half a tile. Use a spirit level to position a guide batten against the last vertical line and nail it.(3)

PLOTTING A HALF TILED WALL

If you are tiling part of a wall, set out the tiles with a row of whole tiles at the top.(4) This is important if you are using REX tiles (tiles with two adjacent rounded edges.

ARRANGING TILES AROUND A WINDOW

Use a window as your starting point so that the tiles surrounding it are equal and not too narrow. If possible, begin a row of whole tiles at sill level (5) and position cut tiles at the back of a window reveal (6). Fix a guide batten over a window to support the tiles temporarily. (7)

MAKING A GAUGE STICK

Mark tile increments
along a gauge stick

SETTING OUT A PLAIN WALL (1-3)
PLOTTING A HALF TILED WALL (4)
ARRANGING TILES AROUND A WINDOW (5-7)

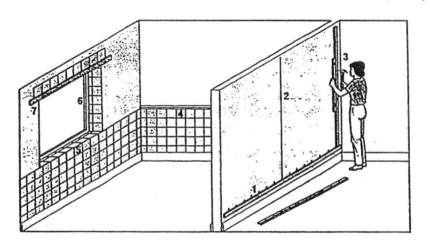

TILING A WALL WITH CERAMIC TILES

It is vitally important that you choose the correct adhesive. Most ceramic tile adhesives are sold ready mixed, although a few need to be mixed with water. The packet or other container should indicate the coverage. A standard adhesive should be suitable for most applications but use a waterproof type in area likely to be subjected to running water or splashing. If the tiles are to be laid on a wallboard, use a flexible adhesive and make sure it is heat resistant for worktops or around a fireplace. Some adhesives can also be used for grouting the finished wall.

Plastic spreaders, usually notched are usually supplied with the adhesive, or you can use a serrated trowel.

HANGING THE TILES

You should spread enough adhesive on the wall to cover about one metre square. Press the teeth of the spreader against the surface and draw it through the adhesive so that it forms horizontal ridges.

Press the first tile into the angle formed by the setting out battens until it is firmly fixed, then butt up tiles on each side. Build up three or four rows each time. If the tiles do not have lugs, place matchsticks, thick card or proprietary spacers between them to form the grout lines. Wipe away adhesive from the surface of the tiles, immediately, with a damp cloth or sponge.

Spread more adhesive and tile along the batten until the first rows of whole tiles are complete. From time to time, check that your

44

tiling is accurate by holding a batten and spirit level across the faces and along the top and edge. When you have completed the entire field, scrape adhesive from the border and allow it to set before removing the setting out battens.

GROUTING TILES AND SEALING JOINS

Use a ready mixed paste called "grout" to fill the gaps between the tiles. Standard grout is white, grey or brown but a range of coloured grouts exist which match various tiles. You can also mix pigments with dry powdered grouts to match any colour.

If you are grouting shower or bath surrounds, waterproof grout is essential. You should use an epoxy based grout for worksurfaces to keep them free of germs.

Leave the adhesive to harden for 24 hours, then use a rubber bladed squeegee or a plastic scraper to press the grout in the joins. Spread it in all directions to make sure all joins are well filled.

Wipe grout from the surface of the tiles with a sponge before it sets and smooth the joins with a blunt ended stick – a dowel will do.

When the grout has dried, polish the tiles with a dry cloth. Do not use a tiled shower for about seven days to let the grout harden thoroughly.

1. APPLY ADHESIVE

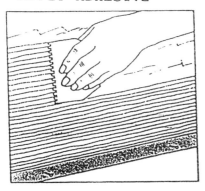

2 HANGING THE TILES

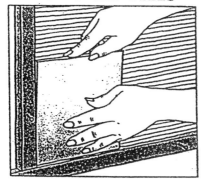

3. GROUTING TILES AND SEALING JOINS

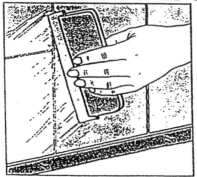

SEALING AROUND BATHROOM FITTINGS

Do not use grout or ordinary filler to seal the gap between a tiled wall and shower tray, bath or basin. The fittings can move enough to crack a rigid seal and frequent soakings can allow water to seep in, create stains and damage the floors and walls. Use a silicone rubber caulking compound to fill the gaps. It remains flexible enough to accommodate any movement.

Sealants are sold in a range of colours to match popular tiles and also sanitary ware. If you are using a tube, trim the end off the plastic nozzle and press the tip into the joint at an angle of 45 degrees. Push forward at a steady rate while squeezing the tube to apply a bead of sealant. Smooth any ripples with the back of a wetted teaspoon.

If you are using a cartridge, snip the end off the nozzle and use the containers finger action dispenser to squirt out the sealant. You can also use ceramic coving or quadrant tiles to edge a bathe or shower unit, or glue on a plastic coving strip which you cut to length.

CUTTING CERAMIC TILES

Having finished the main field of tiles you will have to cut the ceramic tiles to fit the border and to fit around obstructions such as window frames, electrical fittings, pipes and the basin. Making straight cuts is easy using a purpose made cutter but shaping tiles to fit curves takes practice.

TILE CUTTING JIG

This is a worthwhile investment if you are cutting a lot of tiles, a proprietary jig incorporates a device for measuring and scoring tiles The cutter is drawn down the channel of the adjustable guide. The tile is snapped with a special pincer action tool.

There are also diamond cutters, which score the tile enabling you to snap a clean break when scored. This is traditionally achieved by using matchsticks either side of the scored line.

CUTTING THIN STRIPS

A cutting jig is the most accurate way to cut a thin strip cleanly from the edge of a tile. If you do not want to use the strip itself, nibble away the waste a little at a time with pincers or special tile nibblers.

TILING AROUND A WINDOW

Tile up to the edges of a window, then stick RE tiles to the reveal so that they lap the edges of surrounding tiles. Fill in behind the edging tiles with cut tiles.

CUTTING A CURVE

To fit a tile against a curved shape, cut a template from a thin card to the exact size of a tile. Cut "fingers" along one edge, press them against the curve to reproduce the shape. Transfer the curve onto

CUTTING CERAMIC TILES

1. STRAIGHT CUTS BY HAND

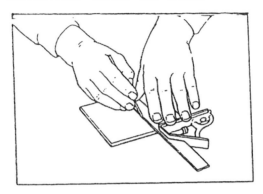

TO CUT TILES BY HAND, SCORE FIRMLY
ALONG THE MARKED LINE WITH A TILE
CUTTER. PROTECT THE SURFACE
UNDERNEATH IF NECESSARY.

2. USING A TILE CUTTING JIG

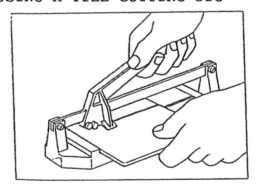

FOR CUTTING PART TILES, A TILE CUTTING
JIG WILL GIVE ANACCURATE FAST CUT. MOST
ARE MARKED WITH DIMENSIONS.

BREAKING THE SCORED TILE

THE SCORED TILE CAN BE BROKEN OVER
A STRAIGHT EDGE OR, MORE EASILY, BY
USING A PAIR OF TILE SNAPPERS.

CUTTING THIN STRIPS

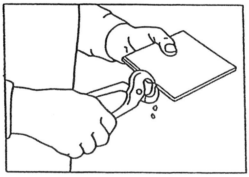

NIBBLE AWAY AT IRREGULAR CUT OUTS
WITH PINCERS (OR PLIERS).

the face of the tile and score the line freehand. Nibble away the waste a little at a time using pincers or a tile nibbler and smooth the edge with a slipstone.

FITTING AROUND A PIPE

Mark the centre of the pipe on the top and side edges of the tile and draw lines across the tile from these points. Where they cross, draw round a coin or something slightly larger than the diameter of the pipe.

Make one straight cut through the centre of the circle and either nibble out the waste, having scored the curve, or clamp it in a vice, protected with softening, and cut it out with a saw file–a thin rod coated with abrasive particles which will cut in any direction. Stick one half of the tile on either side of the pipe.

FITTING AROUND A SOCKET OR SWITCH

In order to fit around a socket or switch you may have to cut the corner out of a tile. Mark it from a socket then clamp the tile in a vice. Score both lines then use a saw file to make one diagonal cut from the corner of the tile to where the lines meet. Snap out both triangles.

If you have to cut a notch out of a large tile, cut down both sides with a hacksaw then score between them and snap the piece out of the middle.

TILING AROUND A WINDOW

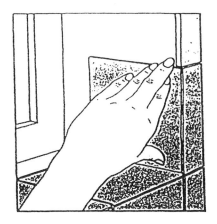

TILE UP TO THE EDGES OF THE WINDOW.
FILL IN BEHIND THE EDGING TILES
WITH CUT TILES.

CUTTING A CURVE

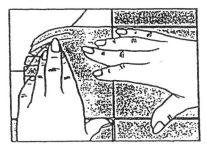

TO FIT A TILE AGAINST A CURVED SHAPE
CUT A TEMPLATE FROM A THIN CARD TO
THE EXACT SIZE OF A TILE. CUT "FINGERS"
ALONG ONE EDGE, PRESS THEM AGAINST
THE CURVE TO REPRODUCE THE SHAPE.

HANGING OTHER WALL TILES

Mosaics

Ceramic mosaic tiles are applied to a wall in a similar way to large square tiles. Set out the wall and use the same adhesive and grout. The mesh backing on some sheets is pressed into the adhesive. The facing paper on other sheets is left intact on the surface until the adhesive sets.

Fill the main area of the wall, spacing the sheets to equal the gaps between individual tiles. Place a carpet covered board over the sheets and tap it with a mallet to bed the tiles into the adhesive.

Fill borders by cutting strips from the sheets. Cut individual tiles to cut into awkward shapes and around fittings. If necessary, soak off the facing paper with a damp sponge and grout the tiles.

Mirror Tiles

Set out the wall with battens but do not use mirror tiles in an area which would entail complicated fixing, for the simple reason that they lack flexibility.

No grout is necessary with mirror tiles. Peel the protective paper from the pads and lightly position each tile. Check its alignment with a spirit level then press it firmly into place with a cloth. Use a wooden straightedge and a wheelcutter to score a line across a tile. Make one firm stroke. Lay the tile over a stretched wire and press down on both sides. Remove the sharp cut edge with an oiled slipstone.

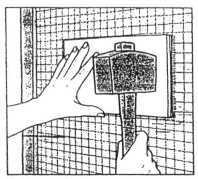

Bedding mosaics
Bed tiles by tapping a carpet-covered board.

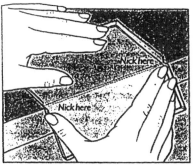

Bending metal tiles

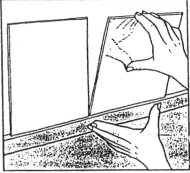

Placing mirror tiles
Position tile before pressing on wall.

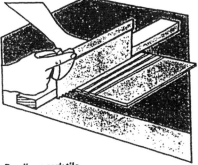

Bending a cork tile
Cut a series of shallow slits vertically down the back of a tile using a tenon saw within the central section, then bend it gently: the slits will enable the tile to assume even a fairly tight curve without snapping, but experiment first.

Add spare pads and fix the tile in place. When this is finished, polish tiles to get rid of messy fingermarks.

Metal Tiles

You should set out metal tiles in the same way as ceramic ones. No adhesive or grout is required. Don't fit metal tiles in dangerous places, i.e. behind electrical fittings. There is a risk that they can conduct current.

Press each tile onto the wall, check the alignment of the tiles regularly, they are not always perfectly made.

Cut border tiles with scissors or tinsnips, but nick the edges before cutting across the face or the surface is likely to distort.

To round over a cut edge, cut a wooden block to fit inside the tile, and align it with the edge. Tap and rub along the edge with another block.

To fit into a corner, file a V shape into the opposite edges then bend the tile over the edge of the table. When the wall is complete, peel off any protective film which may be covering the tiles.

Cork Tiles

Set up a horizontal guide batten to make sure you lay the tiles accurately. It isn't necessary to fix a vertical batten, however. The large tiles are easy to align without one. Simply mark a vertical line centrally on the wall and hang the tiles in both directions from it.

Use a rubber based contact adhesive to fix cork tiles. If any adhesive gets onto the surface of a tile clean it off immediately with a suitable solvent.

Spread adhesive thinly and evenly onto a wall and back of the tiles and leave it to dry. Lay each tile by placing one edge only against the batten or its neighbour then gradually press the rest of the tile onto the wall.

Cut cork tiles with a sharp trimming knife. Because the edges are butted tightly, you will need to be very accurate when marking out border tiles. Use the same method as for laying cork floor tiles. Cut and fit curved shapes using a template. Unless the tiles are pre–coated, apply two coats of varnish after 24 hours.

TILING AROUND CURVES

In many older houses, some walls might be rounded at the external corners. Flexible tiles, such as vinyl, rubber and carpet tiles are easy to bend into quite tight radiuses, but cork will snap if bent too far. Cut a series of shallow slits vertically down the back of a tile within its central section, using a tenon saw, then bend it gently to the curve required.

BRICK AND STONE TILES

Brick tiles are generally used over flat surfaces in order to achieve a "brick" effect. They can look quite authentic if laid in a standard running band. These tiles can be hung vertically, horizontally, diagonally or even in a zig zag fashion to achieve an effect.

SETTING OUT THE SURFACE

Make two gauge sticks, one for the vertical coursing and another to space the tiles sideways. Allow 10mm spacing between each tile for the mortar joints. Work out your spacing side to side so that you have one course of whole tiles alternating with courses containing a half tile at each end. If you are using corner tiles at each end, work out your spacing from them towards the middle of a wall, and place cut tiles centrally. (See 1–6 overleaf.)

FITTING AROUND A WINDOW

Lay tiles vertically above a window in a "soldier course" to simulate a brick lintel

Use prefabricated corner tiles to take the brickwork into a window reveal for the most realistic effect.

CUTTING BRICK TILES

Most brick tiles can be cut with a hacksaw, but if a cut edge looks too sharp, round it over by cutting with a scrap piece of tile. You can also cut tiles using a club hammer and bolster chisel, and the thinnest type can even be cut with scissors.

Fixing brick tiles
Follow this procedure
when fixing brick tiles
to your wall.
1 Plot the tile courses
vertically and
horizontally with two
gauge sticks. Allow joint
spaces between each
tile

2 Use pre-formed tiles
at external corners

3 Set a course of tiles on
end above a window as
a brick lintel
4 Set the bottom row
of tiles on the skirting
on the new wall suface
or substitute with a row
of brick tiles on end

5 Leave a gap for
ventilating the flue in a
blocked off fireplace

6 Fix tiles from the
bottom up, staggering
the vertical joints

GLUEING ON THE TILES

You can, if you wish, use mortar to stick brick tiles to a wall but most tiles of this sort are sold with a compatible adhesive. Use a notched spreader to coat the back of each tile then press it onto the wall.

If you are using pre-formed corner tiles, fix them first, three at a time, alternating headers and stretchers. Check that they are level at each side of the wall with a batten and spirit level then fill in between.

Start filling in by tiling the bottom course, using 10mm wooden offcuts to space the tiles. Every third course, use a spirit level to check the alignment of the tiles, and adjust if necessary.

STONE TILES

Stone tiles are laid in the same way as brick tiles. Coursed stones should be arranged with a selection of small and large tiles for the most authentic look. You should lay the tiles on the floor or other surface before setting out, to plan the setting out, then transfer them to the wall one by one.

Irregularly shaped stones can be laid in any pattern you want, but again its best to set them out on the floor to achieve a good balance of large and small sizes for realism.

With some stone tiles, you have to coat the wall with a special mortar coloured adhesive, which give an overall background, then stick the individual tiles on by buttering their backs with adhesive.

BENDING BRICK TILES

Most brick tiles are made from rigid ceramic but some plastic tiles can be hand bent round a corner or even a curved column. Heat the tile gently with a hot air stripper or hair dryer until it is pliable. Wearing thick gloves, grasp the tile and bend it round the angle.

POINTING THE JOINTS

After 24 hours, use already mixed mortar to point the wall as for real brickwork. Brush smears of mortar from the face of the tiles with a stiff bristled brush. If you don't want to point the joints, simply leave them as they are. The adhesive is coloured to resemble mortar and the joints will resemble raked joints.

THE RENOVATION OF CERAMIC TILES

A properly tiles surface, well finished, should last for many years. However, the overall appearance is often spoiled by damaged tiles., by discoloured grouting or lifting of softer tiles. However, most of these minor problems can easily be solved.

RENEWING THE GROUTING

Instead of raking out old grouting, it is possible to use a renovation kit to brighten up the existing grout. Liquid colorant is supplied in a number of different colours. You should brush this on following the lines of the grout which must be clean and dry. After about an hour, wet the area with a sponge, leave it for three minutes, then wipe off excess colorant from the tiles.

The liquid forms a strong bond with the grout and provides a water resistant finish which can be polished with a dry cloth if required.

REPLACING A CRACKED CERAMIC TILE

Scrape the grout from around the tiles then use a fine cold chisel to carefully chip out the tile, working from the centre. Take care not to dislodge other tiles. Scrape out the remains of the adhesive then clean out the recess. Coat the back of the new tile with adhesive then press it firmly into place. Wipe of excess adhesive, allow it to set, then renew the grouting.

In the next chapter, we will look at the different types of ceiling tiles, and also at the preparation of ceilings, the setting out and the fixing of tiles.

4

CEILING TILES

TYPES OF TILES IN USE

Tiles used on ceilings are usually of the softer variety. Tiling a ceiling is an alternative to papering for disguising a ceiling surface that is rough or cracked. By far the most common type of ceiling tile is made from expanded polystyrene. The tiles are about 10mm thick and either about 300mm or 600mm square. They are available plain or in a range of designs which are embossed on to the surface of the tile. Polystyrene tile adhesive should be used to stick the tiles to the ceiling surface.

Less common are fibre tiles, made by pressing together a mat of wood or mineral fibres. The tiles are rather thicker than polystyrene ones – up to 19mm in some cases – and their edges may be tongue-and-grooved so each tile interlocks with its neighbours. This allows the tiles to be secretly fixed to the ceiling with pins or staples. The surface may be plain or embossed, with sizes gain about 300mm or 600mm square.

To complement a tiled ceiling (or for that matter a paper or painted one) cornice or coving can be fixed in the angle between the wall and ceiling all around the room. Cornices are ornamental mouldings, while strictly speaking, coving is just a curved cross section, linking the two surfaces together. Both types can be formed in situ by plasterers, but nowadays they are sold in pre-fabricated lengths which can be stuck in place and painted.

Cheaper types of tiles are made from expanded polystyrene and should be stuck in place with the same adhesive as that used to fix polystyrene ceiling tiles. They come complete with preformed corners for turning internal and external angles. The more expensive types are formed from plasterboard, fibrous plaster or even glass fibre.

The first two are generally stuck in place with plaster or with a plaster-like adhesive. Glass fibre ones are usually pinned into position.

Another type of ceiling tile is used to make illuminated ceilings. These are supported by a framework of slim, lightweight support members criss-crossing the room just below the existing ceiling level and supported on wall battens fixed round the perimeter of the room. The support lattice carries translucent panels that can be lit from above by fluorescent light fittings fitted to the existing ceiling surface. The panels come in a range of colours and embossed patterns, and can easily be lifted out for cleaning or for maintenance work to the light fittings.

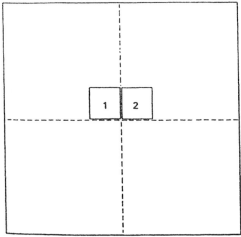

Begin at the centre of the ceiling – you find this by noting the point where the diagonals cross, making allowances for non-rectangular rooms

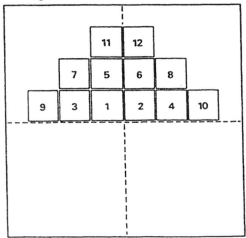

. . . working towards the edge of the ceiling

CUTTING TILES

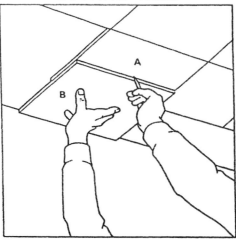

To mark the border accurately, position tile A over the last whole tile and hold tile B over tile A as shown. The uncovered part of A will fill the gap precisely

Cut the tile with a sharp knife. With polystyrene tiles, the cut should go right through; with fibre tiles, snap them over a straight edge

FIXING FIBRE TILES

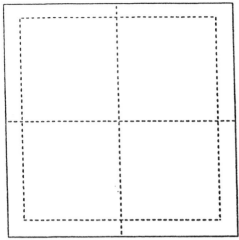

With fibre tiles, you must work out the width of the cut border tiles first and the ceiling must be marked where the first full rows of tiles will be

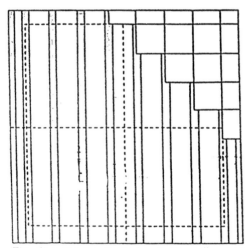

The tiles can be stapled to battens fixed at right-angles to the joists, starting in one corner and working in both directions

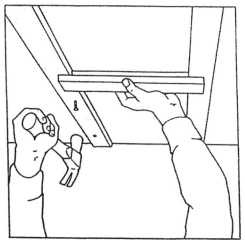

Use a spacer to get accurately repeated gaps between the battens and put nails into the joists above the ceiling – do not nail into plaster or plasterboard

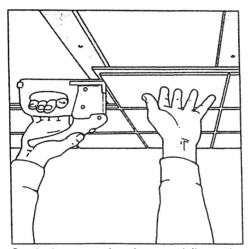

Staple the tongued-and-grooved tiles to the battens through the tongues. The groove of the next tile then fits over the tongue, concealing the staple (or nail)

HOW TO TILE A CEILING

Whichever type of ceiling tile is to be fitted, setting out is the most important factor and, as with ceramic wall tiles, the object of the exercise is to have cut tiles of equal width all round the perimeter of the ceiling.

POLYSTYRENE TILES

With polystyrene tiles, begin tiling at the centre of the ceiling. The first job is to find the centre point by linking opposite corners of the walls with string lines. The intersection marks the centre of the room. Obviously, an allowance has to be made for non rectangular rooms. Next, estimate how many whole tiles will fit in each row across the ceiling. If the border is too narrow, better results will be achieved by either fitting coving round the edge of the room to hide the gap, or if this is impossible, by fixing one tile over the centre point instead of four abutting it.

To stick the tiles in place, coat the backs completely with adhesive, and then simply press them into position. They should not be stuck with blobs of adhesive on the backs as this could increase the flame spread hazard. Once all the whole tiles are in place, work round the perimeter of the room cutting and fitting the border pieces. A polystyrene tiled ceiling can be painted with emulsion paint, but gloss, or any other oil based paint must never be used.

FIBRE TILES

When using tongued-and-grooved fibre tiles, either stick them to the ceiling with panel adhesive (usually used for fixing panels of wallboard to walls) or staple them into place. In either case, start fixing the tiles in one corner of the room, rather than at the centre, so that the interlocking edges can be assembled correctly. This means that the width of the border tiles must be worked out and the ceiling marked exactly where the first row of full tiles comes.

When stapling the tiles, first pin slim sawn softwood battens to the ceiling at right angles to the joists to provide fixing grounds for the staples–they will not hold on plaster or plasterboard. To do this, determine the joist spacing, and mark the ceiling at each joist position. Pin up the first two battens at right angles to the joists, spaced at just the right distance to allow staples to be driven through the tongues of the tiles into the battens.

Fix the first row of tiles to the battens with the grooved edges towards the corner of the room, driving the staples through the exposed tongues. Then cover the tongue of one tile with the groove of the next, and so on to give a secret fixing. With one row completed, add the next row of battens, fix the next row of tiles and carry on in this fashion until all but the last two sides of border tiles are in position.

Cut border pieces and slip them into position before stapling them into the battens. Finish off the ceiling by pinning quadrant beading all round the perimeter, driving the nails into the battens.

ILLUMINATED CEILINGS

These come complete with detailed fixing instructions, but the basic principle is the same in all cases. First, draw a true horizontal line round the room at the level where the illuminated ceiling is to be installed. Then fix the wall support battens along this line, using masonry nails.

Next, install the required number of fluorescent fittings on the existing ceiling. Cut the T shaped support battens to length and rest them into place across the room, from one wall batten to the one on the opposite wall. Finally, drop the ceiling panels into place.

CORNICE AND COVING

This is simply stuck into place using the appropriate type of adhesive. Where pre-formed corners are available, fix these first, and then add full and cut lengths of the cornice or coving to complete each wall. Where mitres have to be cut, fix full lengths from each corner out towards the centre of the wall, and then fill in with butt jointed lengths to complete the run.

In the next chapter, we look at the different types of floor tile in use and the preparation of floors, setting out and fixing of tiles.

5

FLOOR TILES

THE DIFFERENT TYPES OF TILES IN USE

There are a number of tiles which are commonly used for floors. Vinyl tiles are normally used for kitchen and bathroom areas. These softer tiles provide a durable, washable surface and are relatively inexpensive. Tiles are used in place of sheet lino which, of course is easier to lay.

Cork tiles are very popular although this is generally a more expensive method of providing a surface in kitchen and bathroom. Rubber tiles are also used in these areas of the home except they are not so common.

Carpet tiles are used in areas such as the living room. Again, these are used in place of sheet carpet. More common is to find these tiles in offices and industrial settings where a good deal of wear and tear is to be expected.

Ceramic tiles also make a durable surface for floors and can also be very decorative. However, they can also be very expensive to buy and more difficult to lay.

Quarry tiles are the best choice for tough hardwearing flooring that will receive a lot of heavy foot traffic. But beware, they are fairly thick and making even a straight cut is not easy. Reserve them for areas that don't require a lot of complex shaping. Don't lay quarry tiles on suspended wooden floors. Replace the floorboards with 18mm or 22mm exterior grade plywood to provide a sufficiently flat and rigid base. A concrete floor presents no problem, providing it is free from damp. So long as the floor is reasonably flat, the mortar bed on which the tiles are aligned will take care of the fine levelling.

Terracotta or earthenware floor tiles are also very popular but also expensive. They have a mellow appearance and have an ability to adapt to ambient room temperatures. They can be complicated in the early stages of preparation to set out and lay.

LAYING CERAMIC FLOOR TILES

Laying ceramic tiles on a floor is similar to laying them on a wall, although being somewhat thicker than wall tiles, you have to be especially careful when cutting them to fit for neat and accurate results.

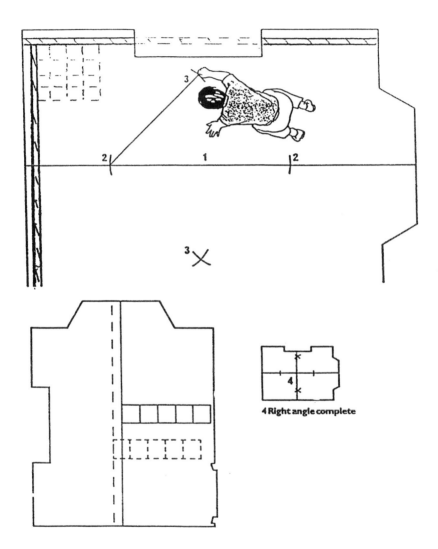

4 Right angle complete

SETTING OUT

You cannot lay ceramic tiles on a suspended wooden floor without constructing a solid, level surface that will not flex. A flat dry concrete floor is an ideal base.

You then need to mark out the floor. Most ceramic tiles can be set out in a similar way: find the centre of two opposite walls, snap a chalked string between them to mark a line across the floor (1). Lay loose tiles at right angles to the line up to one wall. See below left. If there is a gap of less than half a tile width, move the line sideways by half a tile to give a wider margin.

To draw a line at right angles to the first, use a string and pencil as an improvised compass to scribe arcs on the marked line, at equal distances each side of the centre. (2)

From each point, scribe arcs on both sides of the line (3) which bisect each other. Join the points to form a line across the room (4). As before, lay tiles at right angles to the new line to make sure border tiles are at least half width. Nail a guide batten against one line to align the first row of tiles.

If the room is noticeably irregular in shape, centre the first line on the fireplace or the door opening.

Nail two softwood guide battens to the floor, aligned with the last row of whole tiles on two adjacent walls farthest from the door. Set the battens at a right angle – even a small error will become obvious by the time you reach the other end of the room. Check the angle by measuring thee units from one corner along one batten and four units along the other. Measure the diagonal between the marks: it should measure five units if the battens form an angle of 90 degrees.

78

Make a final check by dry laying a square of tiles in the angle.

LAYING THE TILES

Use a proprietary floor adhesive that is waterproof and slightly flexible when set. Spread it on using a plain or notched trowel. The usual procedure is to apply adhesive to the floor for the main area of tiling but to coat the back of individual cut tiles as well.

Spread enough adhesive on the floor for sixteen tiles. Press the tiles into the adhesive, starting in the corner. Work along both battens then fill in between, to form the square. Few floor tiles have spacing lugs, so use plastic spacers or cards.

Check the alignment of the tiles with a straight edge and make sure that they are lying flat by spanning them with a spirit level. Work along one batten laying squares of sixteen tiles each time. Tile the rest of the floor in the same way, working back towards the door. Leave the floor for 24 hours before you walk on it to remove the guide battens and fit the border tiles.

CUTTING CERAMIC FLOOR TILES

Measure and cut the tiles to fit the border as described for wall tiles. Because they are thicker, floor tiles will not snap quite so easily so you will need to buy or hire a tile cutting jig. Alternatively, make your own cutting device by nailing two scraps of thick plywood (12mm) to 50mm x 25mm softwood battens, leaving a parallel gap between them which is just wide enough to take a tile.

Hold the device on edge, insert a scored tile into the gap, up to the scored line – which should be uppermost – and press down on the free end. Snap thin strips from the edge in this way. Saw or nibble curved shapes.

LAYING MOSAIC FLOOR TILES

Set out mosaic tiles on a floor as for ceramic floor tiles. Spread on the adhesive then lay the tiles, paper facing uppermost, with spacers that match the gaps between individual pieces. Press the sheets into the adhesive, using a block of wood to tamp them level. Remove the spacers and then soak and peel off the facing with warm water 24 hours later. Grout as normal.

If you have to fit a sheet of mosaic tiles round an obstruction remove individual mosaic pieces as close to the profile as possible. Fit the sheet (1) then cut and replace the pieces to fit around the shapes.

If you are using mosaics in areas of heavy traffic – a step on the patio for example – protect vulnerable edges with a nosing of ordinary ceramic floor tiles to match or contrast.

LAYING QUARRY TILES

Don't lay quarry tiles on a suspended wooden floor; replace the floorboards with 18 or 22mm exterior grade plywood to provide a flat and rigid base. A concrete floor is ideal, providing that it is free from wet and damp. So long as the floor is reasonably flat, the mortar bed on which the tiles are laid will take care of the fine levelling.

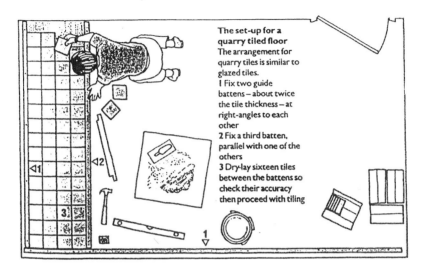

The set-up for a quarry tiled floor
The arrangement for quarry tiles is similar to glazed tiles.
1 Fix two guide battens – about twice the tile thickness – at right-angles to each other
2 Fix a third batten, parallel with one of the others
3 Dry-lay sixteen tiles between the battens so check their accuracy then proceed with tiling

CUTTING QUARRY TILES

Score tile face: tap the back with a hammer

SETTING OUT FOR QUARRY TILES

Set out two guide battens in a corner of the room at right angles to each other, as described for ceramic floor tiles. The depth of the battens should measure about twice the thickness of the tiles to allow for the mortar bed. Fix them temporarily to a concrete floor with long masonry nails. The level of the batten is essential, so you should check with a spirit level; pack out under the battens with scraps of hardboard or card where necessary. Mark tile widths along each batten, leaving 3mm gaps for grouting.

Dry lay a square of sixteen tiles in the angle, then nail a third batten to the floor, butting the tiles and parallel with one of the other battens. Level and mark it as before.

BEDDING DOWN THE TILES

You should lay quarry tiles on a bed of mortar mixed from one part cement-3 parts builders sand. Quarry tiles should generally be soaked with water prior to laying them to prevent them from sucking water too rapidly, when a poor bond could result. Cut a stout board to span the parallel battens. This will be used to level the mortar bed and tiles. Cut a notch in each end to fit between the battens and the thickness of a tile less 3mm.

Spread the mortar to a depth of about 12mm to cover the area of sixteen tiles. Level it by dragging the notched side of the board across. Dust dry cement on the mortar to provide a good key for the tiles, then lay the tiles along three sides of the square against the battens. Fill in the square, spacing the tiles equally by adjusting them with a trowel.

Tamp down the tiles gently with the unnotched side of the board until they are level with the battens. If the mortar is too stiff, brush water into the joins. Wipe mortar from the faces of the tiles before it hardens, or it will stain.

Fill in between the battens then move one batten back to form another bay of the same dimension. Level it with the first section of the tiles. Tile section by section until the main floor is complete. When the floor is hard enough to walk on, lift the battens and fill in the border tiles.

CUTTING QUARRY TILES

Because quarry tiles are difficult to cut you may think it is worthwhile having them cut by a specialist. If you wish to cut them yourself, scribe them with a tile cutter, then make a shallow cut down each edge with a saw file. With the face side of the tile held in a gloved hand, strike behind the scored line with the cross piece of a hammer.

TERRACOTTA TILES

Terracotta or earthenware tiles have long been popular due not only their mellow appearance but also their ability to adapt to room temperature. Whereas, for example, glazed ceramic or quarry tiles remain cold, terracotta tiles are fired to a higher temperature to harden them and this strength makes them suitable for interior or exterior use.

These tiles have natural colour variations. Boxes should be opened and the tiles "mixed" before laying to spread any variation.

SETTING OUT FOR TERRACOTTA TILES

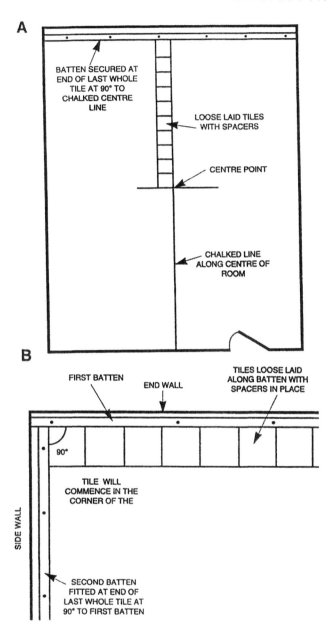

A

BATTEN SECURED AT END OF LAST WHOLE TILE AT 90° TO CHALKED CENTRE LINE

LOOSE LAID TILES WITH SPACERS

CENTRE POINT

CHALKED LINE ALONG CENTRE OF ROOM

B

FIRST BATTEN

END WALL

TILES LOOSE LAID ALONG BATTEN WITH SPACERS IN PLACE

90°

TILE WILL COMMENCE IN THE CORNER OF THE

SIDE WALL

SECOND BATTEN FITTED AT END OF LAST WHOLE TILE AT 90° TO FIRST BATTEN

PREPARATION

It is very important to ensure, as it is with all other tiles, that the surface to be tiled is clean. If there is a sub floor then this must be sound, level and clean, free of dust, grease and any other loose material.

If you are dealing with concrete screed – if this is new screed then allow at least three weeks for the concrete to dry out.

Timber base – make sure that suspended timber floors are strong enough to carry the extra weight of the tiles and if deflection is likely, strengthen with strong exterior grade plywood screwed at 200mm centres into the joists beneath. The plywood should be sealed with wood primer.

If there are existing ceramic tiles they should, if possible, be lifted but, if all of the existing floor is sound, new tiles can be fixed over the old. Glazed surfaces should be degreased, any old polish removed and then roughened with an abrasive disc or sander to give better adhesion.

If other types of floor exist, such as vinyl, cork and linoleum then these should be lifted and if any bitumen or adhesive is left on the floor it will be necessary to use a levelling compound before adhesive can be laid.

Again, as with other floor tiles, it is necessary to secure battening to the floor to provide a good square starting point a short distance away from the real corner. (A+B)

DRY FIXING WITH ADHESIVE

It is important that the tiles are kept clean and dry during laying. If the tiles, after laying, need to be washed, a minimum of three days will be required before the sealing process can be started. The tiles must be kept clean during this period.

It is for this reason that "dry fixing" is recommended. This is achieved by using ceramic floor tile adhesive mixed with the minimum amount of water. This ensures that the minimum water is taken up by the tile, thus ensuring a better bond and a dry tile face, suitable for accepting the sealer once the adhesive is dry.

In general 4mm should be applied to the sub floor using a notched spreader. Then "butter" the back of the tile with a further 2mm. More or less adhesive may be used depending on the irregularity of the sub floor and the tiles, but a solid adhesive bed is essential.

Fixing should be carried out as carefully as possible ensuring that no adhesive remains on the surface of the tiles. Any such marks should be wiped away immediately with a clean damp sponge. Once the tiles are fixed, leave sufficient time, at least 24 hours, for the adhesive to harden thoroughly.

CUTTING TERRACOTTA TILES

Terracotta tiles are extremely hard. We recommend that tiles are cut using a wet cutting machine which can be hired from most shops. This is the safest, quickest and most accurate way to cut terracotta. Alternatively, an angle grinder can be used, after first scoring with a tile cutter. As the angle grinder will create dust, cutting is best done outside.

SEALING TERRACOTTA TILES

The tiles should be sealed after laying so that any marks created will not be able to penetrate the floor surface. However, if any of the tiles are already dirty they need to be cleaned before sealer is applied. Most marks should be easily removed with a clean rag and white spirit but more severe stains may require scrubbing.

For sealing, boiled linseed oil is recommended. This is a natural sealer which enriches the colour of terracotta and continues to harden long after its application. The application of oil can be made with a clean paint brush working it well into the surface. The oil will take about 20 minutes to dry. Within 30 minutes of applying the sealer check that no surplus oil remains on the tiles or dirt will be attracted to these areas. Wipe away any surplus with a clean cloth soaked in a little white spirit.

GROUTING / POINTING

Grouting can begin as soon as the first sealer coat has dried. Tile grout should be applied into the joints of the tiles. It must not be brushed over the tiles. Wipe off any mix which gets onto the surface immediately, with a damp sponge, otherwise staining will occur.

A cement/fine sand mortar mix can be used instead of the tile grout compound and should specifically be used if the tile spacing is over 12mm. It is recommended that you use a semi dry mix of 2 parts cement to 3 parts sand with enough water so that the mortar just binds together in a clenched hand. Mixing the mortar to the right consistency is vitally important. Too little moisture will weaken the finished product, while too much will make a slurry that is difficult to use.

87

When pointing, the mortar should be pushed well down into the joints. The harder it is compacted the harder it will set. A metal pipe of suitable gauge, cut and bent to a convenient size can be used to smooth the joints to a uniform finish. Finally, make sure that any mortar is wiped off the surface of the tiles. A damp sponge can be used to clean the tiles as you work.

APPLYING A FINAL SEAL

Adequate time must be allowed for the grout to set rock hard before the second and final seal is applied. The floor should be thoroughly brushed using a stiff broom to remove the light film of cement dust which will have been left after grouting with mortar. Remove any marks with a clean damp cloth.

Apply the boiled linseed oil to the entire floor, joints included. Within 30 minutes, remove any excess oil remaining on the surface of the tiles with a cloth just dampened with white spirit.

POLISHING

After allowing a few hours for the final seal to oxidise, the floor can be polished with a terracotta wax polish. During the first month or so it is advisable to polish and buff the floor regularly. Thereafter, about once a month should suffice in most domestic situations.

LAYING VINYL FLOOR TILES

Mark out the floor as you would for ceramic tiles. Stack the tiles in the room for 24 hours before you lay them so they become properly acclimatized. If the tiles have a directional pattern – some have arrows printed on the back to indicate this – make sure that you lay them in the correct way. Remove the protective paper backing from the first tile prior to laying, then press the edge against the guide batten. Align one corner with the centre line. Gradually lower the tile onto the floor and press it down.

Lay the next tile on the other side of the line, butting against the first one. Form a square with two more tiles. Lay tiles around the square to form a pyramid. Continue in this way to fill one half of the room, remove the batten and tile the other half.

GLUEING VINYL TILES

Spread adhesive thinly but evenly across the floor, using a notched spreader, to stick about two or three tiles only. Lay the tiles carefully and wipe off surplus adhesive that's squeezed out with a rag.

CUTTING TILES TO FIT

When trimming border tiles, it has to be remembered that edges are rarely square, so cut border tiles to the skirting profile. To make a border tile, lay a loose one exactly on top of the last full tile. Place another tile on top but with its edge touching the wall. Draw along the edge of this tile with a pencil to mark the tile below. Remove the marked tile and cut along the line, then fit the cut off portion of the tile into the border.

CUTTING IRREGULAR SHAPES

To fit curves and mouldings, make a template for each tile out of thin card. Cut fingers which can be pressed against the object to reproduce its shape. Transfer the template to a tile and cut it out. You can also use a profile gauge to mark tiles for cutting complex curves.

FITTING AROUND PIPES

Mark the position of the pipe on the tile using a compass. Draw parallel lines to the edge of the tile, taken from the perimeter of the circle. Measure halfway between the lines and cut a straight slit to the edge of the tile. Fold back the slit and slide the tile into place.

LAYING OTHER TYPES OF SOFT FLOOR TILE

Carpet tiles are laid as for vinyl tiles, except that they are not usually glued down. Set out centre lines on the floor but don't fit a guide batten, simply aligning the row of tiles with the marked lines is sufficient.
Carpet tiles have a pile which must be laid in the correct direction, sometimes indicated by arrows on the back face. One problem with loose laid carpet tiles is preventing them from slipping – particularly noticeable in a large room.

Some tiles have ridges of rubber on the back which mean they will slip easily in one direction but not another. The non slip direction is easily denoted by an arrow on the back of the tile. It is usual to lay the tiles in pairs so that one prevents the other from moving.

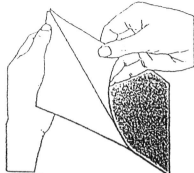

1 Peel off paper backing from adhesive tiles

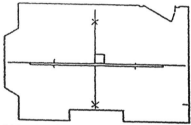

2 Place first tile in angle of intersecting lines

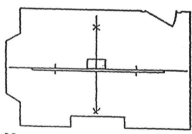

3 Butt up next tile on other side of line

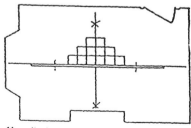

4 Lay tiles in a pyramid then fill in half room

Stick down every third row of tiles using double sided carpet tape to make sure that the tiles don't slide. Cut and fit carpet tiles as described for vinyl tiles.

CORK TILES

Use the methods described for laying vinyl tiles to cut and fit cork tiles, but use a contact adhesive. Thixotropic types allow a degree of movement as you position the tiles.

Make sure the tiles are level by tapping down the edges with a block of wood. Unfinished tiles can be sanded lightly to remove minor irregularities.

Vacuum then seal unfinished tiles with three coats of clear polyurethane varnish.

RUBBER TILES

Use the same methods for laying rubber tiles as for vinyl types. Use a latex flooring adhesive to stick the tiles.

6

USEFUL TIPS

USEFUL TIP 1

Estimating the number of tiles you need is quite simple. Because there are so many different sizes and shapes of tiles, it's best to calculate the area you're going to cover in square metres.

Tiles are usually sold in packs that state the area covered by each pack. This is usually 1–2 square metres for floor tiles and perhaps 2/3 square metre for wall tiles.

It's important to remember that you will need extra tiles to allow for breakages and other accidents during laying, so estimate generously. Also, it's always a good idea to have a few spares in case some are damaged in use. There can be colour variation in different batches of tiles, so it may not be possible to find matching ones later.

To find the area of a *floor*, simply multiply the length in metres by the width in metres. The result is the area in square metres.

If the room is irregular, find the area of alcoves and window bays separately. Then add these to the area of the main part of the floor.

In the same way you can subtract the area of chimney breasts or cupboards where tiles won't be needed.

Finding the area of *walls* is done in the same way. Multiply the length of each wall by the height, and then subtract the areas of doors or windows. Once again, it is better to over estimate slightly.

Then, if you're estimating for *ceramic tiles* you must calculate the number of finished edge tiles to buy (either RE and REX or glazed edge universal).

As you may not know the size of the tiles you will choose, make a rough sketch showing the window or external corners where the edges need finishing. Write the length of these edges on the sketch.

When buying the tiles, substitute the finished edge tiles for field tiles. In other words, if you need 30 RE tiles for an external corner of two walls, buy 30 fewer field tiles than your original estimate.

Remember to allow extra finished edge tiles as well as field tiles.

The packaging of *adhesive* and *grout* always states the approximate area covered by the contents.

USEFUL TIP 2

Resist the urge to begin fixing tiles as soon as you start work. Remember that the result depends most on the planning, so take your time setting out the job and the rest of the work will follow easily.

USEFUL TIP 3

Here's how to remove and replace a damaged ceramic wall or floor tile.

Use a hammer to crack the tile into small pieces, starting from the centre and working outwards. Use only as much force as necessary.

Chip out the pieces carefully with a narrow cold chisel and club hammer. Be careful not to damage the edge of the adjacent tiles.

When all the pieces are removed, chip away any adhesive and scrape away grout from the edges of the space. Vacuum out the dust and grit.

Dry lay the new tile to be sure it fits and that there is room beneath it for the adhesive.

Fix the tile and allow it to set before grouting.

USEFUL TIP 4

To remove and replace a cork, rubber or vinyl tile, use an old wood chisel and a hammer.

Pierce the tile in the centre and work outwards, being careful not to lift the edges of adjacent tiles. Use a stiff scraping knife to remove the old adhesive, and vacuum the space well to be sure it's clean and free of debris. Now lay the new tile.

Apply the correct adhesive and bend the tile as you fit it into the space. It helps to warm vinyl tiles for a few minutes to make them more pliable.

Then press down firmly, from the centre toward the edges, to remove air bubbles.

USEFUL TIP 5

To drill holes in ceramic tiles for fixing towel rails, etc., you should use a slow speed electric drill and a masonry drill bit. Mark the position of the hole with a felt tip pen, and stick clear adhesive tape over the mark. This helps keep the drill bit from slipping off the mark as the hole is being started.

Use the drill at the lowest speed and apply only gentle pressure.

If you insert a plastic plug into the hole to take a screw, push the head of the plug completely through the tile, into the wall. That way there is no chance of cracking the tile when the screw is tightened.

USEFUL TIP 6

Be sure to use the right tile and adhesive for the job. Wall tiles for walls and floor tiles for floors and work surfaces or anywhere strength may be needed.

Use heat resistant tiles, adhesive and grout on fireplaces and kitchen work surfaces. Also, on surfaces where food is prepared, make sure the tiles have a non lead glaze and that the grout is non toxic and non stain. Special kitchen work surface grout is available.

Use frost proof tiles, adhesive and grout on exterior walls, patios, steps etc.

Use water proof adhesive and grout on areas that are often wet, such as shower cubicle walls and floors.

Finally, for any surface that is slightly flexible, such as chipboard (particle board) lined walls, plywood panels or hardboard covered wood floors, you must always use a flexible wall or floor tile adhesive.

USEFUL TIP 7

If the grout on wall tiles becomes stained, it may be possible to clean it by rubbing it gently with a pencil eraser.

If the grout is too discoloured to be cleaned. use a nail to scrape out the old grout. Be careful not to damage the edges of the tiles.

Use a brush or vacuum cleaner to remove the dust and then regrout the tiles.

USEFUL TIP 8

Where the edges of tiles meet a bath tub, sink or work surface, use silicone caulk instead of grout. This will remain flexible to absorb movement and resist staining. Make sure the gap to be filled is clean, dry and free of grease.

Apply the caulk direct from the nozzle of the tube, working in this direction.

Then smooth with a wet finger and remove any excess immediately with a damp cloth.

USEFUL TIP 9

To fit quadrant tiles around a bath or basin, always work toward the centre of each wall from the ends.

Fix the mitred tile in the corner and the round edge tile at the other end of the row. Then fix whole plain tiles until there is a gap left in the middle. Cut a plain tile to fit, leaving the correct gap either side.

USEFUL TIP 10

When the tiling is finished follow the manufacturers' instructions concerning the sealing and maintenance.

Cork floor tiles must be sealed with polyurethane varnish unless they are ready sealed by the manufacturer.

Unglazed ceramic floor tiles and vinyl tiles must be sealed with the correct proprietary sealants recommended by the manufacturer. Although rubber floor tiles are not usually sealed, some have a protective layer of wax that must be removed with a cloth dampened with white spirit (mineral spirits).

SAFETY TIPS

- When cutting tiles with a spike or trimming knife, make sure the tile is well supported and that all parts of your body are out of the way.

- Wear gloves or use barrier cream to protect the skin of hands when working with cement, adhesives and grout.

- Keep sharp tools, adhesives, grout and all products away from children and pets.

- Don't wear a tie or loose clothing when using power tools.

7

SPECIALIST WORK

CARING FOR VICTORIAN HOUSES

As many people who have bought a Victorian house have discovered, areas of these houses are tiled with very attractive tiles (if they have not been the victim of "modernisation"). However, a number of questions are posed by the existence of these tiles, many often in need of restoration. This chapter looks briefly at the history of Victorian domestic tiles and then offers practical advice on restoration and maintenance.

TILES IN VICTORIAN HOUSES

As we have seen, the use of tiles became very popular during the Victorian period. Decorative tiles first arrived in the Victorian house by covering the floor. The porcelain manufacturer, Herbert Minton had revived the old tradition of "encaustic" tile making which is a specific design process involving stamping a design into the body of a plain clay tile while it is still damp and filling the design with clay of a contrasting colour. Minton then supplied these to the aristocracy and helped to establish them as *the* fashionable floors to have. These tiles were expensive and were often combined with quarry tiles and geometric tiles in order to cover large areas at less cost.

Geometric pavements were restricted to those areas that were seen by visitors to the house; garden paths, entrance halls and conservatories. Kitchens, sculleries and passages seen only by the servants would have cheaper floors made up of six inch square quarry tiles, either in plain red or red tiles alternating with blue-black tiles. Walls of plain glazed tiles (or of glazed brick) were installed in response to new building regulations. The relative grandeur of tiled schemes in different parts of the Victorian House was closely related to the status of different rooms; present-day manufacturers design expensive and elaborate tiles for kitchens, but the Victorian householder would have considered these inappropriately extravagant.

In wealthier households, the provision of bathrooms and lavatories gave more scope for tiling walls. An extremely elaborate tiled scheme for Gledhow Hall, Leeds was devised by Burmantofts in 1885, in which every inch of the bathroom-the coffered ceiling, the pedimented chimneypiece, the arcaded walls and the elaborate dado, is clad in glazed ceramic. This was, of course, exceptional., but in many lesser houses, a tiled dado of at least four feet high and with a moulded ceramic top rail was installed-a hygienic innovation that reflected the modern attitude to sanitation.

In the public parts of the house, tiles were used to draw attention to noteworthy features of the architecture. From about 1870, tiled porch dadoes began to enliven entrances. Manufacturers offered landscape and floral panels for visitors to study while they waited for the door to be opened. The tiled dado might be continued into the entrance lobby.

Fireplaces were the natural home for decorative tiles in every class of Victorian house. Entire chimneypieces made out of glazed ceramic were on offer for wealthy customers, but in most cases, the tile decoration was restricted to a pair of framed panels in the reveals or "cheeks" flanking cast iron fire surrounds of the 1870's and after, which could be filled with any standard six inch tiles.

Fireplace tiles were accurate mirrors of contemporary taste; all developments in fashionable interior decoration were studied by tile manufacturers, who rushed out appropriate designs to complement them. Floral bouquets were perennial favourites, sunflowers in blue and white pots adorned the fireplaces of Aesthetic interiors of the 1880's and various historical revival styles all had their day. Designs would be matched to the rooms in which they were used; perhaps flowers in the drawing room, scenes from shakespeare in the study, Aesops fables in the schoolroom, and childrens games in the nursery. The manufacture of tiles for nursery fireplaces was a flourishing branch of the industry in the last quarter of the nineteenth century.

The decorative hierarchy was as strictly observed in fireplace tiles as in other elements of the Victorian interior. Reception rooms had the smartest tiles, often in panels. Bedroom fireplaces also had decorated tiles, but these were more likely to be in sets of five identical tiles. In lesser bedrooms and the kitchen, the fireplace would have plain glazed tiles.

Tiles were also incorporated into furniture. They appeared as splashbacks in washstands, waterproof tops on tables for conservatories, and as decorative elements in hallstands, chairs and sideboards.

So many millions of tiles were produced that a certain standardisation of designs was inevitable. Large firms had in-house studios to supply designs for tiles, and most tiles were designed by anonymous artists, but some were the work of well known designers, including A W N Pugin, William De Morgan, J Moyr Smith, Kate Greenaway, CFA Voysey and Walter Crane, and have become sought after by collectors.

Most tiles used in Victorian houses were mass produced, but the high value that the arts and crafts movement placed on making things by hand led (in the better off households) to a rejection of the standardised designs of many transfer printed tiles and a revival of hand painting techniques. William Morris designed simple decorations of stylised flowers, painted by hand in the traditional blue and white colours of old Delft tiles. He produced his first lustre tiles in about 1870. Inevitably, mass produced tiles were adapted to cater for this change in taste, and firms such as Minton's were soon producing printed tiles in imitation of the hand painted variety. The types of tile that are most commonly found in Victorian houses are:

ENCAUSTIC TILES

As we have seen, encaustic decoration is achieved by stamping a design into the body of the plain clay tile before firing while it is still damp, and filling the design with clay of a contrasting colour.

The tile is then fired to fuse the two clays together. In 1830, Herbert Minton bought a share in a patent for making encaustics by machine and began to develop the process. His first encaustics, limited to red and buff colours, were for churches and bore ecclesiastical motifs, but within a few years, the Minton catalogue included designs suitable for civic buildings and for houses, in a much wider range of colours, and several rival manufacturers had entered the market.

GEOMETRIC TILES AND QUARRIES

Geometrics are small, shaped tiles that can be combined in a variety of patterns to make hard wearing floors. Dozens of shapes and sizes were available, all based on subdivisions of a six inch square tile, and the catalogues of the major manufacturers contained several pages of suggested arrangements for geometric pavements. Most geometrics were of natural clay colours, but white, green and bright blue were also available. They were used for hall floors, hearths and gardenpaths. The name "quarry" (A corruption of the French *carre* meaning "square") refers to any undecorated, unglazed clay tile.

GLAZED TILES

Glaze is the hard shiny finish applied to the surface of a tile to make it durable. The final appearance of the tile can be altered by adjusting the opacity of the glaze, or by adding chemicals to colour it. Slight variations in the density of coloured glazes create a more pleasing "moire" effect when plain glazed tiles are combined across large areas of wall, and should not be regarded as defects.

RELIEF DECORATION

Damp clay or clay dust can be pressed into a mould to produce raised ares on the tile surface. During firing, the liquid glaze runs into the depressions, creating pools of darker colour that enhance the three dimensional effect of the design.

TRANSFER PRINTED TILES

Most decorated tiles produced in the Victorian period were transfer printed from a dark outline design printed onto tissue paper which might then be coloured in by hand before glazing and firing. Lithography made it possible to print flat area of colour directly onto the tile surface, removing the necessity for any painting by hand.

TUBE LINED WALLS

Tube lining involves outlining a simple design on a plain tile using a soft clay or slip sneezed through a narrow tube-exactly like icing a cake. The spaces within the outlines are then filled with coloured glazes and the tile is fired. The technique lends itself particulary well to large panel pictures, since the strong lines carry the design well from one tile to the next, and to the sinuous lines of Art Nouveau designs. The effect of tube lining can be mimicked by dust pressing, and many tiles with simple coloured motifs were produced at the turn of the century.

RESTORATION AND MAINTENANCE

Before any cleaning materials and methods described below are attempted on a large area of tiling, it is recommended that a small test patch, on a single tile, in an unobtrusive spot, be cleaned.

CLEANING FLOOR TILES

Regular detergent floor cleaners will take care of day-to-day cleaning. To remove ingrained dirt, use a specially formulated product, such as BAL Ceramic floor cleaner or HG Systems Extra Cleaner: follow the manufacturers instructions closely and wear goggles, gloves and protective clothing if necessary. Scouring powder should never be used on tiles. Although cleaning products will help to shift a great deal of built up dirt and wax, be prepared to contribute a lot of elbow grease.

Tiled floors that have been covered with sheet flooring are often disfigured by the remains of mastic adhesive. This can be removed with a solvent such as HG Tarol. Surface dirt can be scraped off by using a paint scraper of the kind that holds a Stanley knife blade in a plastic handle. This keeps the blade at an acute angle to the surface of the tile, avoiding scoring or gouging actions which will damage the tile surface. Green scouring pads can be used with a gentle circular movement to clean unglazed tiles. Steel wool or wire brushes should never be used on tiles.

REPAIRING TILED FLOORS

The tiles in geometric pavements are usually so closely packed together that they are impossible to loosen unless they lift up of their own accord. However, since the small unit size of the tiles often causes these pavements to fail in sections, only patch repairs, carefully matched to blend into the surrounding tiles, may be required.

In halls, the central strip suffers most from heavy traffic; in garden paths, it is frequently the edges, vulnerable to heavy rainfall and encroaching grass, that break up. If many of the small tiles have been broken or lost altogether, it may be possible to retain the original tiles and reduce the cost of the repair by redesigning the pavement, using the remaining original tiles in a border pattern around a central panel of new plain quarries, or vice versa.

Geometric tiles are still being made and the art of laying elaborate geometric pavements is enjoying a revival. However, for patch repairs to an existing pavement, it is usually best to look for plain, six inch square tiles of the right colours which can be cut to the shapes and sizes required. Patience will be required in the search for a good colour match; a meticulously cleaned sample of the original tile should be used as a guide, and the old and new tiles should be compared under both natural and artificial light. Differences in the surface texture of unglazed tiles are just as noticeable as differences in colour, since they affect the way in which the tiles reflect light. Most modern tiles are thinner than Victorian ones, so it may be necessary to build up the substrate below the patched in tiles with extra cement, to take account of this difference.

Where tiles have lifted themselves, the cement left behind bears the imprint of the tile backs. This should be gently chipped away in order to give a good key and room for the new cement. In recent years, the fashion has been for wide bands of grouting, but in Victorian and Edwardian floors, the tiles were set very closely together, often with the thinnest possible line of grouting. Geometric tile pavements in particular rely for their effect on close butted tiles laid with their edges touching. In floors of one colour, the plain quarry tiles were often laid in staggered courses, offset like brickwork, or diagonally, rather than in the square grid pattern favoured today.

FLOOR FINISHES

The traditional treatment for a tiled floor after cleaning was to apply warm linseed oil. This was wiped over the floor in a very thin slick and left so that it could be absorbed into the unglazed surface of the tiles. It would be followed by a coat of wax polish. This gave a stunning, lustrous finish to the floor, but it is so labour intensive to apply and maintain that it is inappropriate in most modern circumstances.

Before the finish can be applied, all the old wax and oil has to be cleaned away. Linseed oil tends to yellow once it is exposed to light, and unless the wax seal is rigorously maintained, the oil also attracts dirt. Modern cold polishes, for example johnsons Traffic Wax, are perfectly adequate.

On no account should tiled floors be varnished or sealed with any kind of resin based or polyurethane finish. Besides giving a completely inauthentic, synthetic appearance, these may cause long term problems by sealing in damp under the floor.

CLEANING GLAZED TILES

Since glaze prevents dirt from penetrating the body of the tile, most glazed tiles are relatively easy to clean, but care must be taken not to damage the glaze. Loose dirt can be washed off with warm soapy water, and the tile washed to a shine with a soft cloth. Never dunk a tile into boiling hot water, as this can cause a tile or its glaze to crack. Dilute household bleach can be used to remove dirt that has worked its way into fine cracks or crazing, but only after soaking the tile in plain water (use a water can to "shower" fixed wall tiles). This prevents the dry clay from absorbing the dirt once it has been dissolved into the bleach. Iron stains appear as rust coloured patches on the tile surface. They can be removed with a rust remover such as jelonite (sold for car maintenance). Tiles that have been painted over can be cleaned up with a proprietary paint stripper such as Nitromors.

Never scape the surface of the tile with a sharp implement or scratchy material such as steel wool. A knife blade scraper, held at the correct acute angle, is useful. White scouring pads, designed for use on non stick pans, are ideal for working on stubborn dirt. Use a soft scrubbing brush or an old toothbrush to work away built up dirt from relief or tube lined tiles. Take particular care when cleaning the surface of tube lined tiles, as it is all too easy to chip or break the fine lines of clay which stand proud of the tiled surface. Glaze decoration (which can be recognised by its matt appearance when the tile is tilted against the light) and gilding require expert cleaning. To remove old cement from the back of a tile is difficult, and should

To remove old cement from the back of a tile is difficult, and should never be attempted on a valuable tile; the chipping action of a chisel can easily shatter the whole tile. This risk can be reduced by laying the tile face down on a tray that has been filled with sand to a depth of at least two inches; the sand will absorb most of the shock. A heavy build up of cement can be removed by using an angle grinder held at an acute angle to the tile surface. The tile must be firmly clamped, face down in a vice or work mate, before any work with an angle grinder is done. Wear a mask and goggles to protect against cement dust.

REPAIRING GLAZED TILES

The degree of damage to glazed tiles depends greatly on where they were used.. Tiled dadoes outside front doors may suffer from frost damage; hearth tiles were often cracked when fire irons were dropped on them; any kind of relief tile-mouldings, edging and corners-is particularly vulnerable. Tiled walls tend to escape accidental damage, but may have been deliberately scarred for the installation of new wiring and plumbing.

Damage such as drill holes can be made good with a filler such as polyfilla, smoothed to finish flush with the surface of the surrounding tiles. Left white, this is a neat and honest finish, but it can also be painted to blend into the surrounding area, using acrylic paints and glazes. Small repairs to chipped edges and mouldings can be carried out with a polyester resin and painted in the same way. Where deep mouldings (for example, on ceramic chimneypieces and architraves) are damaged beyond repair, it may be possible to remove the damaged unit and replace it with a short length of wooden moulding cut and painted to match.

As with floor tiles, it is important to mimic Victorian styles of layout and grouting: plain tiles were usually offset like brickwork, or laid diagonally. Grouting was generally used in the thinnest possible line. New grouting can be coloured to match the old by mixing it with universal stainer (an oil pigment sold in tubes and available from good paint suppliers). These stains become lighter incolour as they dry, so do a test patch first to check the colour match before grouting a large are.

FINISHES FOR GLAZED TILES

In most cases, the glaze itself is the only finish required. However, to enhance the shine and further protect the surface of glazed tiles in a vulnerable area such as a porch or hearth, a microcrystalline wax may be used.

BUYING TILES

Architectural salvage outlets can be a useful source of original tiles, provided that you buy with care. Look for clean tiles, with no cement adhering to the back, clean edges and no chips. Crazing of the surface need not impair the practical functioning of the glaze; unless it is so bad as to distort the colour or the pattern, it gives character to the tile. Often, tiles that have been stacked in a shed or in the open air are very dirty; insist on seeing them washed or wiped, so that you can assess any damage before buying. Some Victorian tiles have become extremely valuable, and there are antique dealers who specialise in tiles for the collectors market.

Some manufacturers will make new tiles to order, to match Victorian originals, and most manufacturers produce new tiles for the Victorian house market. Some of these are precise reproductions of nineteenth century tiles; others are disappointing pastiches in Victorian style. It is a good idea to shop around and compare the ranges on offer. Do not rely on photographs in glossy magazines, but ask to see samples of the tiles themselves before buying. Remember the hierarchy of decoration in Victorian houses; grand effects should be reserved for entrances and reception rooms, so resist the temptation to create a more elaborate tile scheme than is appropriate for the room, or for the status of the house

USEFUL ADDRESSES AND PLACES TO VISIT

Thanks are given to the Victorian Society for letting me reproduce sections of their publication "Caring for Victorian Houses". The Victorian Society are active in promoting the restoration, and preventing the needless demolition, of Victorian and Edwardian houses, including tiles in these houses which are very often beautifully designed and laid out. Lectures, walks and tours are organised for members. The Society is a registered charity and benefits from covenants. For further information, contact the **Victorian Society**, 1 Priory Gardens, Bedford Park, London W4 1TT. Tel: 0181 994 1019.

OTHER ADDRESSES

Heritage Tile Conservation Ltd
Unit 1, Stretton Road Industrial Estate, Stretton Road, Much Wenlock, Shropshire TF13 6AS.
Tel: 01952 728157

Jackfield Tile Conservation Studio
Jackfield Tile Museum, Ironbridge, Telford, Shropshire TF8 7AW
Tel: 01952 883720

Tiles and Architectural Ceramic Society
Membership Secretary, Reabrook Lodge, 8 Sutton Road,
Shrewsbury SY2 6DD.

This is the national society responsible for the study and protection
of tiles and architectural ceramics.

PLACES TO VISIT

Gladstone Pottery Museum
Uttoxeter Road, Longton, Stoke on Trent ST3 1PQ
Tel: 01782 319232

Leighton House Museum and Art Gallery
12 Holland Park, London W14 8LZ.
Tel: 0171 602 3316
Contains an Arab Hall, created in 1877 to accommodate Lord
Leighton's collection of Islamic tiles and many tiles by William De
Morgan.

Minton Museum
London Road, Stoke on Trent
Tel: 01782 319232

Standon, East Grinstead, West Sussex RH19 4NE
Tel: 01342 323029

Arts and Crafts House decorated by William Morris

William Morris Gallery
Water House, Lloyd Park, Forest Road, Walthamstow E17 4PP
Tel: 0181 527 5544

Collection of William De Morgan and Morris & Co tiles.

All titles, listed below, in the Straightforward Guides Series can be purchased online, using credit card or other forms of payment by going to www.straightfowardco.co.uk A discount of 25% per title is offered with online purchases.

Law
A Straightforward Guide to:
Consumer Rights
Bankruptcy Insolvency and the Law
Employment Law
Private Tenants Rights
Family law
Small Claims in the County Court
Contract law
Intellectual Property and the law
Divorce and the law
Leaseholders Rights
The Process of Conveyancing
Knowing Your Rights and Using the Courts
Producing Your own Will
Housing Rights
The Bailiff the law and You
Probate and The Law
Company law
What to Expect When You Go to Court
Guide to Competition Law
Give me Your Money-Guide to Effective Debt Collection
Caring for a Disabled Child

General titles
Letting Property for Profit
Buying, Selling and Renting property
Buying a Home in England and France
Bookkeeping and Accounts for Small Business

Creative Writing
Freelance Writing
Writing Your own Life Story
Writing performance Poetry
Writing Romantic Fiction
Speech Writing

Teaching Your Child to Read and write
Teaching Your Child to Swim
Raising a Child-The Early Years

Creating a Successful Commercial Website
The Straightforward Business Plan
The Straightforward C.V.
Successful Public Speaking

Handling Bereavement
Play the Game-A Compendium of Rules
Individual and Personal Finance
Understanding Mental Illness
The Two Minute Message
Guide to Self Defence
Buying a Used Car
Tiling for Beginners

Go to:

www.straightforwardco.co.uk